THE BASTARD CHILDREN
OF
DHARMA BUMS

Joshua Michael Stewart

to my Japhy, Scott Graves

Published by Human Error Publishing
Paul Richmond
www.humanerrorpublishing.com
paul@humanerrorpublishing.com

Copyright © 2020
by
Human Error Publishing & Joshua Michael Stewart
All Rights Reserved

ISBN: 978-1-948521-42-0

Front Cover:
&
Back Cover

Joshua Michael Stewart
&
Human Error Publishing

Author photo, Chanel Dubofsky

Human Error Publishing asks that no part of this publication be reproduced or transmitted in any form or by any means electronic or mechanical, including photocopy, recording or information storage or retrieval system without permission in writing from Joshua Michael Stewart and Human Error Publishing . The reasons for this are to help support publisher and the artist.

WELCOME

the honking
     of geese

               lingers

in gray sky
     long after shadows
        scrape
the roofs of our houses

          s
          i
          n
          k

your teeth into the light
     that squeezes
out of my window
     stuff your mouth
with cornbread

Where Is Stuff

The Bastard Children of Dharma Bums 1-34	11

The Hardest Path — 53

Pioneer Valley	54
Nature Lesson	55
April 2018 - April 2020	61
Snow Clouds Gather like Dust Balls Under an Old Couch	63
Double Cherita	64
Po Chu-I Golden Shovel Poem	65
Spurts and Flashes	66
Sitting at a Picnic Table at the Quabbin Reservoir	70
Ignes Fatui	71
Ryokan Golden Shovel Poem	72
Shelburne Fire Tower	73
If I Had a Hammer...And Some Nails...And Some Wood	77
Po Chu-I Golden Shovel Tanka	78
A Message To Su Dongpo	79
To Life	80

"The Bastard Children of Dharma Bums"

are 'sculpted poems,' essentially erasure poems without the erased lines, taken from each chapter of Jack Kerouac's The Dharma Bums. I manipulate the lines, punctuation, and in some cases, the tense of a word, changing "breaking" to "break," for an example, but otherwise the words within each poem are as they fall within Kerouac's Novel.

The Bastard Children of Dharma Bums

1

Hopping a freight,
  duffle bag under head,
     knees crossed,
    clouds roll north—
      intend sleep.

Relax thin old bum,
   jump a bottle of wine,
    devote devotion,
      believe in tranquility,
   believe wandering.

Whip out a prayer,
  announce death,
  shower roses
on modest little life,
    surf the mountain.

Cold and foggy,
  we spent the warmth of God.
    Farewell, Saint Teresa,
      the night in my blanket,
        the voice in the void.

2

Deep in the woods,
interested in Indian lore,
idealistic anarchism, play

the guitar and sing
old work songs, zipping
barefooted, suffering,

howling his poem, drunk,
incomprehensible,
urging love to eat.

3

Rose-covered backyard,
porch vines, tomato plants,
cool October nights.

Little kitchen gas stove,
hot water, pillows and mattresses,
swinging Ella Fitzgerald album.

Peaceful cup of tea, steaming.
High on nothing, calm and warm,
sick of the big city. No rain

among white clouds, I face
my dark ravines.

4

buy a bicycle—
throw poetry against
screaming glass

5

This was love-making
    in rubber boots.
She was casual at the typewriter.
    I wasn't mad about love,
and she looked white as a pillow.
    Facing the Temple
of Hurt, kissing her with delight,
my Buddhism naked,
    she realized stars
give strength to people
    living in weeds.

6

High mountain in late afternoon,
I took shoes. What about food?
I've got your sleeping bag,
bread to eat back in the city.
I'm bringing those cold stars
and stir in the snow, diced
vegetables, dried prunes,
fix us for 24 hours.

Primitive fire howling
wilderness ecstasy,
mysterious mountain.
Talking America,
God, gun, murder:
starlit, petrified Jesus.

7

The oddest friends wake up on the south coast,
a roaring red over the hill. We ate bread and cheese
in morning freshness, the sun warm, the bread baked,
the cheese sharp, a good breakfast suddenly gone.

Under juniper trees, we drank sunlight slanting down
snowcapped mountains in the distance. I poured
conversation. We washed it down with far-off looks
back home, that highway as it runs through Carson City.

8

Trackless snow along a white farmhouse,
dogs bark through the void.

Li Po getting drunk on God—drinking
a whole new way of living.

I'm sick of civilization.
We can't drive back home.

Maybe it won't be so cold tonight,
I'll light a bonfire by nightfall.

Past adventures bless my boyhood.
Grave eyes cry like birds.

9

I felt like lying down in the woods and face
a long-dead dream, forgotten song drifting

across childhood, past manhood, all the living
and the dying, the heartbreak. Sleep here, tonight.

We might wake up tomorrow. I remember rambling
amongst pines, gurgling creeks. A mountain

is a Buddha sitting perfectly still. I drink my life,
drink more—let the world boil, get hungry.

When I opened my eyes the stars were aching,
nothing there to soothe the night wrapped in night.

10

I rousted, got kindling for the fire.
I was hunting huge logs. Brewed
a fresh pot of tea. Stars blaze,
vast Milky Way. The altitude
enough to get you drunk.
Woke up under huddled darkness,
my breath, warm. These wet socks.

11

In the afternoon a wind rising.
Afraid of falling down,
I was in no hurry to scramble

these rocks of Matterhorn
before nightfall. Landslides,
little avalanches—terrifying

under huge planetary space.
Clouds immense, vistas
distant. Oh, what a life

this smashing song of joy—
the sweat, the human dust.

12

    lonely

          moments

dark in the woods

      singing hysterical

killing silence
    black-as-pitch

          slept dead

    woke up a child

13

Wondering if I heard
the gas station payphone,
my fingers chatter
with a jug of wine.
The astonished poet—
a hip girl in love
with Whitman,
refuses to subscribe
to the privilege
of consuming crap
and making children,
writes poems wine-soaked
and wild, praying cops
and the Republicans
learn how to wake up
and start breathing.
I sleep good, live cheap,
and don't give a shit
for all that machinery
in a house. I got songs
made up plucking
on strings tucked away
in my brain. We walk
on both sides of the street
not hurting anyone.

14

Avoid sweet-dead salvation.
Walk the streets among

dusty shirts and zippers,
all kinds of rubber boots

and sleeping bags.
Walk in the Apocalypse

with a frying pan and tin cups.
Pluck out fire like a new man.

15

Slung it on to San Francisco,
all fascinated
hunting speeches
about mankind,
    skeletons, and sins.
We're all going to be arrested—
    live with some old knife
        in the kitchen, staring
at new revolution police
    swooping down on
everybody in Long Beach,
everybody in Greenwich Village.
    It's only the beginning,
but believe in dedication to dream.
    We're all asleep
at the roof's edge.
   The sidewalk six flights below.

16

Wander like Ma Rainey
with her howling voice,
breaking blues beautiful.

Preach Hell in Heaven
to drunk kids
interested in Buddhism.

Trying to see with eyes closed
the ghost slips slow
into my shoes

and jump off a freight
that rolls in the raw night
of industrial America.

17

Rolled hot up the road
to San Jose to catch freights.
Cop cruising cars—I aimed
for the river, ran like a criminal,

crashed out sweating, stomped
deep in streams, hesitated
till dusk. I spread my sleep
on leaves. My head felt sad

like night-fog. I cried
a homeless-man reason to cry
in the underbrush. I am a prayer
tumbling down the highway.

18

The song I kept singing long on the other side of Riverside was "Christmas on Main Street." Thin in my mind that night, I peed on a small fire. With the big pack on my back, ambling foothills, I walked, smiling. I ate a bowl of soup, a big can of pork and beans. I drank shots of tequila, was bleary, wasted, but excellent. Cars zipped up New Mexico, cut through Las Cruces to Alamogordo, drove in beautiful Indian country, New England meadows, and me in my blazing silence, woke in the morning, eager to hitchhike to North Carolina. Got impatient, walked to the bus station for the next bus to West Virginia. Dusk over Blue Ridge Mountains. I walked freezing streams, drifting snow, naked railroad tracks. Gray-blue dreams stomping across my mother's yard. I looked at the dog trembling in the cold. I unleashed him.

19

Oil burning stove on the back porch,
winter-barren cottonfield, pinewoods,
good-old-sleeping-bag winter nights,
my head buried in duck-down warmth.
Strode out in the moonlit frost,
worn out a little path, meditated under
a favorite pine. I bowed, clasped hands
in moonwhite. Dog barking, big trucks
rolling, freight trains going north.
Fell into a trance, my body sunk
into peace. Went back to the house,
warmed by fire. Slipped a bottle,
enjoyed midnight-cathedral ministering
doctrines in lacey snow, my cat blessed
on my lap—a little saint light. The world
bursting with beautiful poetry,
I went to bed with Emily Dickinson.

20

Meditation studies bear fruit, late January.
Frosty night, dead words forever, forever.

Big dogs yell to the stars, wise serene spirit
awaken forever, forever. Thank you, sperm

and bones. Sudden desire strong among streams.
Myself, yes, shining warmer in the woods.

Porch stars wet in the sky. I'd been half-asleep
in ephemeral dreams. I am emptiness.

Grow through suffering in rambling fields.
Hard-working men know my mortal voice.

21

Spring came.
　　　Heavy rains.
　　　　　Puddles
　　　　　　　everywhere.
　　　　　　　　　Winds whipped snow.
　　　　　　　　　　　Beauteous moon.
　　　　　　　　　　　　In the pines
　　　　　　　　　　　　　my nephew took
　　　　　　　　　　　　　from the ground
　　　　　　　　　　　　　a pine cone
　　　　　　　　　　　　　and he said,
　　　　　　　　　　　　"My head
　　　　　　　　　　　and my eyes
　　　　　　　　　　a poem."
　　　　　　　　　The pine tree
　　　　　　　　whispers birds.
　　　　　　My quiet heart
　　　　　leans against
　　　white spruce.
　I lost my Dharma
on a well-worn path.
Happy dogs
 swallow
　　my Dharma
　　　　under cloudy moon.
　　　　　　The world
　　　　　　　looking for Heaven,
　　　　　　　　poor, pitiful Heaven.
　　　　　　　　　I bless all living
　　　　　　　　　　creatures ecstasy.
　　　　　　　　　　　Sitting in straw
　　　　　　　　　　　　I think nothing,
　　　　　　　　　　　Just dream strange
　　　　　　　　　　ghostly Buddhism.
　　　　　　　　　I sing, "You're Learning
　　　　　　　the Blues," as I'd go

to my woods
with my dogs,
accept sun in grass.
I'd go back
to the well-traveled path,
see Buddhas hiding
in the woods.
I sit without food,
my mother calling
from the back porch,
beg me to pity
a sad bootless dream.
Fingering juju beads,
I pride my kindness
to animals. My pain—
tender drama
in time and space.
I laugh more than listen.
All things empty,
made to be unmade,
ghosts afraid to
exist.
What does it
mean
sitting
under stars
throughout
emptiness
and awakeness?
I felt compassion
for the trees
because we didn't argue.
The dogs perk
up their ears,
lick my face.
In the woods
I'd stare
existence away.
I'd stare
in all directions.

As some lone weeds
    blossom,
        I'd dream the words
            came to an end.
            I'd dream
                transcendental visits
                    under flowers.
                        I saw the Buddha
                            who never said anything.
                                I remember the vision
                                was devoid of sensation,
                            pure egolessness.
                    Form is emptiness
                emptiness forever.
    The dead cry out
 over rooftops,
announce glorious
simple truth. I'm going
  to the lone land
    and gay streets.
        My awakening
            sweet weird bliss.
            My life
                glowing empty.
                I wanted
                    a white flower
                        with small petals.
                            Rub it on her neck—
                                a nurse I knew.
                                I was too interested,
                                    a little scared
                                    of transcendental
                                    grace.
                        I pitied forgiven men
                        the worst righteousness.
                "Don't let the blues
                  make you bad,"
            sings Sinatra.
        On my final night
    in the woods

there was nothing to do,
    nothing kissing goodbye.

22

In Corte Madera, California,
a wooden cabin built
on a steep grassy hill covered
with eucalyptus and pine,
built by an old man years ago,
I live there as long as I want.
Good woodstove, kerosene lamp.
Live the solitary life. I sit,
smoke a pipe, drink tea,
hear wind beat
eucalyptus and cypress.
During winter, hitchhiked
Northwest through Portland snow—
a week in a berrypicker's cabin.
Excited in my mind, crystal vision
of my childhood, but I looked to rain
on the road, rested under roofs
of hardware stores, drank wine.
Thought of sleeping by the tracks,
but cops kept circling. I slept in a hotel
and in the morning I got a ride to Atlanta,
picked up by a fat broad-brimmed hat
who drove fast. Tried to sleep,
but kept waking up. Louisiana,
then Texas oil fields. Ride ends—
El Paso, arriving at midnight.
I walked straight for the railroad yards,
stretched my bag behind the tracks.
That night dreamt the most beautiful sleep
behind lines of boxcars,
imminent mountains in starlight.
Morning, I discovered the sky flawless,
had pork and beans, a royal breakfast.
Contemplated a twenty-five-cent locker
in the railroad station, then walked the city,
sauntered in the bars—too many drinks
and smoke, got sick, excused myself,

but didn't want to leave. Walked
through El Paso, out to the station,
got my bag out in the moonlight,
realized I learned how to cast off my soul.
I meditated in the desert winter night.
The mysterious roar roaring the roar of birth.

23

In the morning I had eight dollars cash.
   Went to the highway, jumped railroad

     fence. Kept low, waited. I climbed
train, rode out of L.A. with grass stem

in my mouth. Went to Santa Barbara,
   went to beach. Had food over woodfire.

     My destiny—to die on the Midnight Ghost.
I got on a flatcar, spread my bag,

my shoes a pillow. Woke up mid night.
   Woke up dreamless. The trip swift.

24

Live joyous, America!
Study Buddhist, wander
barefooted baking bread.

Walk a mile, gentle creature.
Play records, work carpentry.
Put a few dollars generous
in the dinner communal.

Bring the stars to butterfat grass.
Singing crows leave the world grateful.
My wind howled desolation.

Reading geology by mirror, a poet
talked of ladybug-lightning storms.
Lightning danced flowery,
hunting the mountains.

Starvation bites me. I discovered
Zen freedom. I'm tired of money.
I'm tired from meditating.

Morning sun out and butterflies
pouring in through old Dharma.

25

Chant in Buddhist monasteries.
Take refuge in the Dharma.
Take refuge in scrambled eggs.

Eat your pancakes. I'll show
you how to handle Zen.
Christine came out in the yard,

swinging down the smell
of butterflies in the grass.
The Buddha came to a puddle,

wallowing in mud-Truth.
In the kitchen, having attained
nothing, Li Po realizing

it was all empty, played records
and lounged around smoking.
Then Christine sat in the grass

writing haikus, watching
the afternoon go to bed and dream.
We called Beauty, who worked

as the janitor. The Buddha picking
a lute, singing, "I was hitchhiking
with a mind full of devils,"

smiled and danced.
In the morning, I took Dharma
on the trails in the wandering

meadow on horseback. Angels
swimming through the void
of tall trees began to jiggle

mysterious sun against my eyelids.
As a blue hummingbird yelled
a greeting, buzzing wings,

my joy got down on knees,
talked to the beautiful flowers
and to a sprig of pine needles.

Then, like a laughing crow,
turned and went staggering
over the side of the hill.

26

A mischievous boy, I tried to talk
to the fancy ladies in lawn hats.
Having to smile real nice, I felt

like a dead crow. I wrote a poem
to a crazy woman. It was hard to live
up to angels sitting cross-legged

in holy snow. I opened my eyes
like windows, peering out into the night
across the valley, digesting stillness.

27

I don't feel like singing
with an ulcer.
I drink joy.
I drink
   your belly sick.
I could float across
   downtown Oakland
to find enlightenment
lying in the street.
At dusk, the Buddhists
drink saki
   out of teacups.

28

The night I could hear God smile a big smile.
That night flowed warm and pleasant. In the yard,
fire spread hungry poetry in my mouth. That night

a ghost began dancing, leaped up and whirled
around a bonfire. I began to dance myself. The night
where madmen wandered, squealing down the road

to Oregon woods. That night Honor stomped off
drunk in the sweet grass. The night the stars, hearing
me sing, yelled back dull and empty witticisms.

29

The morning sprawls
golden spirits in the woods.
I weather mountain fog,
scroll and unfold like a river,

climb lonesome hills,
poetize the burning world
to amuse God. I plunge

into a glades' fresh sun
and talk with mossy frogs
along a dozing creek.

During the night
Dostoevsky's ghost sings
in meadows with cows,
dedicates prayer to a flower.

30

Hand-grasping exhausted, we
  a meadow, we a mountain, trudge
    green afternoon and fawn grass.

We deep in dust, struggling
  in barbed-wire boots, stomp
    flowers like Neanderthals,

climb burden's darkness.
  Child and father in the woods,
    waiting to love love's end.

31

I don't need sadness talking
about how I had the heart
of a gravel truck, a face

deliberately run off the highway.
I spatter beer on the wild desolations
of the world, huddle against

the big red neon wet dreams
of America outside a skid row hotel,
gulp deep in the belly, a torrent.

32

An old man roils
    downstream
  to eternity,   ululating
    Truth
                    beyond

    emptyspace   blue,

  a   sun   river,   all   downpour   waves.
takes coldish up   riding   that   of

The old-timer remembers a Chinese girlfriend
      down in Seattle,
        singing songs with his guitar
    as waves plash
        against wishes,
    lash and thrash in mist.

            underbrush,
        rocky   wet skin
      up   brushed
    climb   by rocks,
  hard   afraid
 a   of the
In   steepness,

      curse
      God,

finally entering alpine meadow with switchback trails,

         he drops beaten-faced
                  on a patch of tiny flowers,
                        gulps
                  rain-stained dust,
                        showing his long teeth
                              in all directions.

33

In morning-blue sunshine, snow-covered timber
and cream clouds in panorama, I have nothing
to do but rest in grass, glory before me. Drinking

tin-cup water, I sing, "I'm happy as darkness,
a snowman stalking a crackling fire." I meditate
facing imaginary Han Shan in alpine grass.

Strange ideas walk this dream—
let the mind be bugged, eye all horizons.
My eyes—shooting stars in the Milky Way.

34

Raspberry Jell-O in the setting sun
poured through unimaginable craigs.
Rose-tint hope—brilliant and bleak.
Ice fields and snow raging mad.
I read snowy air and woodsmoke.
The wind dark, clouds forge.
The sing in my stovepipe absorbs
vaster, darker storm closing in
like a surl of silence. No starvation
turmoiling. My shadow the rainbow
I haloed. Your life a raindrop.
I stood in rose dusk, meditated
in half-moon thunder.
My mother's love drenching rains
washed and washed.
I called Han Shan in the mountains.
I called Han Shan in morning fog.
I closed my eyes, yelled dark wild
down in my garbage pit.
My hair long in the mirror.
My skin soaking pristine light.
My fire roaring. I hear the radio
singing, "She was the wind
which passes through everything."
"Birds rejoicing sweet blueberries
for the last time." Sitting, I twisted
real life and cried cascades
answering the meditation bell.
I know desolation.
I owe gritty love back to this world.

THE HARDEST PATH

PIONEER VALLEY

my heart's the cow refusing
to come in for the night
the lazy clunk of its bell
accompanies your breath
in the lightless pasture

NATURE LESSON

Spring's been cold and rainy, so on the first cloudless day, I hop in the Corolla, and travel west to the Seven Sisters Mountain Ridge in Hadley, Massachusetts, for a late morning hike. It'll feel good to be in the mountains again after a long winter of not venturing far from home, with the exceptions of work and the grocery store, I've pretty much been in hibernation.

> spring
> I paw sleep
> out of my eye

I stop at a pharmacy, purchase the most expensive, all-natural insect repellent they sell, then quickly get back on the road, take Route 9 past the Quabbin Reservoir, through Belchertown and Amherst, then park in a dirt lot off of Route 116, across the street from one of the trailheads. I spray myself from boots to buzz-cut with the insect repellent, and strap on my backpack.

> wildflowers
> all I smell
> is cedar

White rectangles painted on tree trunks lead the way. It's not long before I'm winded and sweating profusely. There are steep rocky pitches where I have to use my hands to scramble up the trail. My backpack contains my journal and a few thin volumes of poetry, but nothing that should make the trek so difficult. Did I choose the hardest path? I stop and rest on a small bluff looking eastward, the modern buildings of UMass Amherst, look out of place within the landscape of plush hills and quilted farmland. Ice-age glacial sheets helped form these mountains, and a prehistoric lake, Lake Hitchcock, once covered much of the valley. I read a few Gary Snyder poems, and as I scratch in my Journal, sweat drips from my brow onto the page. The constant pop, pop, pop, from the gun range below echoes off trees and boulders.

> lake hitchcock
> what was written
> now illegible

I climb to the summit. It doesn't take long, maybe a half-hour. However, it's not the peak I meant to reach. I thought I was climbing the eastside of Mount Holyoke, which I've climbed several times before, but from the west. The Summit House, an old hotel perched on top of Mount Holyoke, can't be seen from where I'm standing. I'm sure I know how to get there, but that would mean climbing down one mountain to climb up another. The hike up to this point has been exhausting, I'm not going to consider the notion. I find a granite slab to plop down on, it's warm from the sun, but there's shade from a pine. I chomp on an apple I had stashed in my pack. I whip the core over a rocky overhang, and think far too late that there might be hikers below.

I can't see it, but I know the Connecticut River flows between this mountain and the city of Northampton. Because of a few pines and bushes, I see mostly sky, and possibly far off to the northwest, Mount Greylock. Others took advantage of the good weather, and snap photos or munch on granola bars or raisins packed in sandwich bags. I exchange pleasantries with a few, but mostly keep to myself. The truth is, I wish I was back home, writing poems or picking my banjo while the cats sleep on the bed and rocking chair as traffic, birds, and rustling leaves lull me from outside the windows. This happens often: I putz around the house feeling antsy, then push myself out the door to go to a coffee shop or bookstore, or mountain, and once I get there, I want nothing more than to race back home.

> wrong mountain
> a black and yellow butterfly
> lands on my pant-leg

A young woman walks down a path on the north side of the mountain. She moves quickly—it looks easier than the way I came up. I head in her direction. I know I'll need to get to the east side of the mountain, but there must be a trail that branches off of this one. The trail slopes downward, and there are the same white rectangles blazed on the trees. I don't want to creep the woman out by following too closely, so I take my time getting to my feet, but now she's nowhere in sight, and the path begins to climb uphill. The terrain's rugged. At times, you have to go up to get down, but this keeps going up and up, and before I know it, I reach another summit. I don't know what to do, except I know I don't want to turn back. There's a sign with an arrow: To Chmura Road. WARNING: unmarked and confusing trails.

> unfamiliar path
> a garter snake slithers
> through the understory

I've never heard of Chmura Road, but it's a road, which means it's off the mountain. Much of the trail is deep with mud and ruts. I no longer hear traffic or gunfire from the shooting range. On at least two occasions I discover mounds of scat too big to be from a dog, and too small to be from a horse. I look over my shoulder for bears.

I empty onto Chmura Road, and look left, scan right. A residential street with expensive homes and manicured lawns. A high school kid rides by on his mountain bike. I ask if he knows how to get to Route 116.

"116?!" There's surprise in his voice and he needs to pull out his phone for a map. "Well, if you head north, you'll eventually hit Bay Road, that'll lead to 116."

I know Bay Road. I know how far it'll be until it connects with Route 116. "Okay, will heading south be shorter?"

"Oh yeah, it should," he says, "but the thing is, I wouldn't know which trails to take."

It's shorter. I thank him, turn south, and start walking. The road is long and I'm tired. My feet hurt. I don't own hiking boots, all I have are steel-toe construction boots, and my big toe rubs against the metal plate where the padding inside has worn away. I don't come across any side streets, and wonder what the kid meant by "trails." I soon find out when the road comes to a cul-de-sac surrounded by oaks. That is, except for a gap between two trees, a path that leads back into the woods.

> sound of a lawnmower
> mosquito buzz
> in my ear

No trail markers, but there is a fork that heads east. The sound of traffic returns and is somewhere in front of me. It has to be Route 116. I walk for a while; the trail spills out into an open field. The grass is about four feet tall, and there's a small hill that prevents me from seeing the other side. I start to cut through the field. A dog barks, the barking gets louder, closer. I don't know if I'm trespassing on private property, and I sure as hell don't want to get mauled, so I turn back.

> lost in the mountains
> smell of cow shit
> civilization near

It's been forty-five minutes since I re-entered the woods from Chmura Road, four hours since I descended the first summit. I take another unmarked path. It ends in someone's backyard, but I know the house, at least I've driven past it before, I know the road it's on, Bay Road, just a little farther up from where I would've been if I just walked the opposite direction on Chmura Road. I stagger out from behind a garage, and in the driveway, a guy works on his truck engine. I don't acknowledge him. He glances at me, then turns back to his socket wrench.

> everywhere
> green leaves and brown bark
> lady slipper

I walk two-and-a-half miles up Bay Road, the sun beats down on my scalp. There are no trees along the road. I've got a large Thermos of water I've been reserving in my backpack. I stand off to the side of the road, unzip my pack, and take four big ice-cold gulps as family-crammed cars and commercial trucks throw warm wind in my face.

>sunbaked road
>honking horns
>cricket chirps

I make it to Route 116 with about a half-mile to go to where my car is parked. Out of the corner of my eye, on the other side of the guardrail, a rabbit chews on grass. It watches me for a moment, then turns and hops into the underbrush. Besides a garter snake, a few birds, and some insects, this is the only wildlife I've seen all day.

>rabbit under
>proceed with caution sign
>beer cans in the weeds

I reach my car, collapse on the driver's seat, drain what's left in my water bottle, and drive the thirty minutes home. Inside my apartment, I sink into my swivel chair to peel off my muddy boots. I hesitate, frightened of what condition my feet are in—am I going to have a sock full of blood? I'm sure I've got a blister begging to burst. I slip off my damp socks and discover only a small blister under my big toe. I pull off my shirt. There's a deer tick firmly attached under my left armpit. I pluck it off and flush it down the toilet. Lyme Disease crosses my mind, but I'm too spent to think about it.

Days pass. I don't see the infamous bulls-eye rash. A week later, I wake up with a headache. I diagnose myself as going through caffeine withdrawal since I haven't had my coffee yet, but after my third cup, I still have a headache. I must be dehydrated. I drink water, pop a couple of Advil.

Memorial Day. I help a friend plant his garden. We rip weeds out of the ground, aerate the soil before we plant carrots, tomatoes, pole beans, swiss chard, peppers, onions, and herbs like basil, rosemary, and dill. While we work, I tell him about my mishap on the mountain. Later, we drink cold beer on his porch, shake our heads in disgust as we talk about our President, and watch my friend's two young daughters play in the yard.

       empty water gun
       two clouds slug
       across the sky

The next morning I'm achy, especially in my shoulders and neck. It feels like someone whacked me with a 2x4. I must be getting old, or I moved the wrong way when tilling the garden with a pitchfork. I'm freezing. Another cold spring morning. A hot shower will revitalize me. I walk into the bathroom, and catch myself in the mirror above the sink, see a bullseye rash under my arm. My thermostat reads seventy-four degrees. I'm shivering. I'm not cold, I have the chills. I'm not sore from gardening, and the headache had nothing to do with a lack of coffee. It's Lyme. I call my doctor; the receptionist fits me in for a late morning appointment. I strip off my boxers, and step inside the shower. As the water massages my sore neck and back, I think about all the indoor activities I can do during the summer.

       air conditioner
       birch leaves rustle
       outside the closed windows

APRIL 2018 – APRIL 2020

spring rain
he's told no one
he's going blind

                                      autumn rain
                                      the outside cat
                                      finally comes inside

winter shadows
rabbit tracks in the snow
between tombstones

                                      snow-patched hillside
                                      a doe and two yearlings walk
                                      between white pines

april morning rain
a finch with red plumage
bursts from the porch eaves

                                      inside a tulip bulb
                                    a hummingbird
                                    from behind, my love
                                    sticks her tongue
                                    in my ear

rippling stream
a crow hops
from rock to rock

summer morning
a goose swims
on its reflection
I no longer ask why
I'm blessed with friends

july dawn
a flock of geese rise
off the still lake

summer morning
I slide a board in the dumpster
to free a raccoon

yellow leaves
drop into the river
flow over the falls
you've been gone ten years
our love gone longer

what mistakes
are quarantined
I walk the lake
even crows
are silent

SNOW CLOUDS GATHER LIKE DUST BALLS UNDER AN OLD COUCH

Suppose God doesn't own our souls
but rents from the Devil. We believe
what we can bear. An old man brings

his dead wife's dress to his face
despite it scented with another man.
A woman with pine-needle hair shouts

into a payphone that had its cord cut.
And my shadow on the wall gesticulates
like a king addressing his peasantry.

DOUBLE CHERITA

mother's day

the disease
has taken her voice

through the phone
her quick breath
nursing home clatter

**

morning
rain

deleting
my mother's
number

out of my phone

PO CHU-I GOLDEN SHOVEL POEM

I cannot unlearn to swallow
honey-glazed peaches, call shadows
anything but, brother. I'll shake
boughs sugared with years of snow, toss out
the cat, shoo it homeward
to kin, offering in mouth. Beating wings.

SPURTS AND FLASHES

This morning, I wake knowing I want to go to the New England Peace Pagoda in Leverett, Massachusetts, but also know I'm not in a hurry. I have my daily dose of two cups of coffee (black) while I scroll through Facebook, test my blood sugar, eat a bowl of Raisin Bran, and take my morning pills. I get dressed and feed the cats. I let the calico in through the bedroom window and scold her for staying out all night by bringing her to my chest and forcing her to endure my cuddles and kisses.

>crisp morning
>the cat's fur smells
>of pine needles

I drive to the Quabbin Reservoir, park my car, and take my morning walk on the Winsor Dam. The dam is half a mile long, one of the longest dams on the east coast. I walk the length of it six times which takes little more than an hour. It's an uneventful morning. The sky's a deep blue with a few lazy clouds, and the same three turkeys I see every day, graze in the grass below the dam. The lake's more choppy than normal, and down from the turkeys is a flock of Canada geese of about three adults and nine goslings. Once, about a month ago, I was trekking back to my car when a moose stepped out from the birch and oak, and stood right in front of me. I froze, couldn't believe what I was seeing. The moose didn't move, but looked right at me. It was larger than any deer, but not as large as most bull moose, and it didn't have antlers, so it must've been a female or a juvenile. I slowly walked backward, chanted under my breath, "Holy shit, holy shit, holy shit." After a few seconds, the moose proceeded to the other side of the woods, gone as quietly as it had arrived.

>a moose steps
>onto the path
>the same paralyzing fear
>as when I had to stand
>before my father

I head west on Route 9. I eventually reach the winding roads of North Amherst that roll into Leverett. I've been to the Peace Pagoda a handful of times, but I still get lost. I know I don't want to find myself on Route 63. At every turn, I plead for it to not be Route 63, but eventually, just past the Route 63 sign, I pull my car over to the side of the road. I drag an old TomTom out of the glove box. It takes a few minutes to get it working, but soon I'm back on the road and after a few minutes I turn into a gravel parking area.

I walk for about five minutes on a path through the woods. At the end of the trail, the canopy of trees opens up to a lush green field, blue sky, and in the center, the white dome of the Peace Pagoda. On the left, made from tan and white stone is a Buddhist temple. It has large windows and two lion statues flanking the steps leading to its large wooden doors. I've never been inside the temple. I've been reading up on Buddhism for years, and I practice mindfulness, but I don't feel comfortable calling myself a Buddhist, like I haven't earned it or something. I feel that if I set foot in the temple I'd be trespassing, and I don't want to give any sense of disrespect, so I go no further than the steps. I look back toward the field and the path that led me here. I look toward distant blueish-gray mountains, listen to crickets and birds, and think, I could live here—just walk into the woods and disappear. I'd be okay with that.

> in the woods
> fantasy of a life
> of solitude
> the distant sound
> of a freight train

There's a walkway that circles the pagoda—at each of the north, south, east, and west points of the dome there's a Buddhist statue painted gold. I'm thankful that such a place exists so close to home. There's a pond a short distance from the pagoda that has beautiful pink water lilies. Goldfish swim just below the surface, and at the water's edge is a bright-green frog with yellow eyes, it doesn't move, and for a long while, neither do I. A stone bridge crosses the pond, and near the bridge is a small tree that once had a wasps' nest in it. I'll tell my sweetheart that the nest is no longer here, but I know she'll never return.

> peace pagoda
> my love walks too close
> to the wasps' nest

As I cross the bridge, I start to think about my meditation practice. From January 2018 to April 2019, I meditated every day for twenty minutes without missing a single day. I'd sit in a straight-back chair with my eyes half-closed either in silence or with some jazz playing softly. Most of the time I'd just focus on my breathing and observe my monkey mind as objectively as possible, other times I might do a body scan or a guided meditation, but in the past four months I haven't meditated at all. I still work on mindfulness, while doing the dishes, driving to work, or out on my morning walk, but it's not every day, and I don't set a timer of any kind—I do it more in spurts and flashes when it comes to mind, especially when I'm anxious or find my thoughts spiraling down an abyss of negative thought-stories.

On the other side of the pond, a rock garden, and strung from tree to tree are brightly colored prayer flags. On one of the tree branches are some wind chimes ringing out the familiar notes of a pentatonic scale. There's no dramatic reason for why I stopped meditating, it just seemed that over time it became one more thing I had to do, one more chore. I'm a counselor. I work in a residential program for adults with special needs. I often work twelve-hour shifts where there aren't twenty minutes to sit and meditate, and if I do try to squeeze it in somewhere, I spend the whole session worrying if the office phone is going to ring, or if one of the clients will knock on the door needing help with something, and in the end, whether I was able to get through the twenty minutes uninterrupted or not, I'm more stressed and frazzled than I was going into it. I do miss it, and I may start up again, but I don't think I'll be so rigid with making sure it's done every day for a specific amount of time, and then berate myself for being a failure at living up to my own expectations.

> late morning
> here to hear it or not
> the cicada sings

I sit on a wooden bench, watch two bumblebees do what they do on goldenrods that live next to some pussy willows. I focus my attention on the bees, then on the movement of the goldenrods in the wind, then the wind on my face, then on my breathing, uninterrupted.

> prayer flags
> flutter above
> yellow zinnias
> I leave footprints
> next to the pond

SITTING AT A PICNIC TABLE
AT THE QUABBIN RESERVOIR

Muddy bird prints on the pine-board top.
I want them to belong to eagles or hawks,
but convinced they're of duller feathers.

I'm unschooled in avian tracks,
but read that the Chinese alphabet
was inspired by fowl feet in snow.

There's a rustling behind a boulder
and from behind appears a ruffed grouse.
It clucks, pecks at the ground.

Shaped like a football awaiting kickoff,
it struts my way on three-pronged toes
that match the impressions on the picnic table.

I zoom-lensed skyward, scoped autumn canopy
for falcon, vulture, other birds of prey
and here in reddish and copper plumage,

the thing I tried to find in a raptor's soar,
hops next to me on the bench
and stares up with one brown eye.

IGNES FATUI

Latin for something deluding or misleading. Literal translation: "foolish fires."

What you've mistaken for a monocle
is a dewdrop dangling from my eyelash.
And what you thought were semaphores
zigzagging in the field last evening
was the pell-mell of newly winged angels.
I play, "My Guitar Wants to Kill Your Mama,"
on a pyrite-plated kazoo, interchanging guitar
with kazoo of course. Are you dazzled
by my caterpillar-skinned leotard?
When I Watusi are you left breathless?
I am the wisteria under your window
which you take as a slow fire engulfing
your house in purple and white flames.

RYOKAN GOLDEN SHOVEL POEM

We were ghost, breath, and wind
all at once. We took
pleasure in everything that pleased us.
We knew how to keep darkness away,

our life a fire at the edge of waves.
Our switchblade history—the bond we've kept.
The cold bodies that sleep between us
keep our lips from drifting apart.

SHELBURNE FIRE TOWER

November 11, 2019, Veteran's Day, my friend Scott and I are going to hike up to the Shelburne Fire Tower. I'm up by 4:00 a.m., take a quick shower, check my blood sugar, and have a bowl of Raisin Bran so I've something in my stomach for when I take my meds. The weatherman says it'll be around forty degrees today, but it's always colder in the mountains, and who knows how windy it'll be. I'm a firm believer in the adage, better to have it and not need it, than to need it and not have it, so I put on my long johns underneath my jeans and red and blue flannel. I fill my Thermos with water, pack my camera and notebook, and I'm out the door by 6:45 a.m.

> snow clouds quilt the sky
> three cats warming
> the warm bed

Scott and I have known each other since seventh grade. In high school, we co-lead a jazz group, and though we haven't played in a band together in over twenty years, the harmonic memories of those times will forever keep us in rhythm. These days, we live an hour away from each other, and our work schedules couldn't be more opposite. It's a rare thing for us to have the same day free from other obligations.

I drive north-west to the town of Greenfield. I meet Scott in a parking lot behind a bank, and after exchanging pleasantries, I pop my trunk so he can transfer his backpack and trekking poles from his car into mine. We travel west on Route 2 toward Shelburne. It doesn't take long to find the trailhead about 50 yards past the turnoff into Shelburne Falls, a village famous for its old trolley bridge that's been turned into a floral garden.

> bridge of flowers
> an old friend's hand
> clasped in mine

The trail starts off steep, and I'm soon out of breath. Scott hikes more than I do, and moves a lot quicker. In a short time he's a good distance ahead of me. The air's brisk. I can feel it deep in my lungs, and my throat's dry. Every few feet there are laminated signs nailed to trees letting hikers know what kind they are, and a bit of description, including an illustration of their leaves. We stop for a breather, and as I learn the Latin name for red maple, Scott notices some princess pine peeking out from the undergrowth. "This used to grow all around my meme's cottage," he says. "People would go around and collect them to make wreaths and other Christmas decorations, but no one mentioned to us kids that we shouldn't pull them up by their roots or when they're about to seed, and by 1985 they were all gone."

> november's gray wind
> the pursuit of happiness
> stuck in our boot treads

We continue toward the summit. My body has acclimated to the climb. I'm no longer out of breath and, not to say the hike is easy, I'm not feeling the strain on my thighs and knees as in the beginning. However, I'm sweating right through my long johns and flannel, so much so, my jeans are damp to the touch.

Scott tells me that his wife, Christine, is getting certified to be a yoga instructor. I ask how his daughters are doing in school, and mention the book I'm reading, a true story about this twenty-year-old kid who one day drove into central Maine, parked his car, and didn't come out of the woods, or speak to another human being for twenty-seven years. My envy echoes off the quiet birch that surrounds us.

> bare trees
> the only sounds of wildlife
> are our voices

We reach the top of Mt. Massaemett. There's a clearing with a couple picnic tables. In the center is one of only two stone fire towers in New England. It was built in 1909 and stands at sixty-five feet. We lay our packs and trekking poles on one of the picnic tables and sit for a few minutes. I even take off my Vermonter-style black and red plaid coat that's wet around the collar with sweat. I take a few hard gulps of water from my Thermos, and watch steam rise from my skin.

The fire tower doesn't have a door so you can walk up the spiral staircase. Without a door, and the fact that it's made of stone makes it look like a cave, which is why I half-jokingly ask Scott if he thinks a bear might use it for its hibernation. We chew this gristle for a moment, but then conclude that it's more likely that we'd stumble upon a raccoon, opossum, or even bats. Despite all this, we decide to venture inside the tower.

> dark, cold, damp
> I reach out not knowing
> what it is I touch

Scott has a headlamp and leads the way, but because of the twisting staircase, Scott's headlamp proves useless to anyone who is behind him. There's a steel railing, but it's ice cold and I can only hold on to it for a short amount of time before it becomes a piercing pain to my palms. There are a few rectangle windows that allow enough gray light to make out the narrow steps. We're unable to reach the absolute top of the tower because there's a locked door, I'm sure the forest rangers don't want people messing with any maps or equipment, but we go as high as we can, and from our viewpoint we can see into Vermont and New Hampshire, and down into the heart of Shelburne Falls. I can see the buildings of downtown, the two bridges that cross the Deerfield River. The cars parked along the streets could be mistaken for Matchbox Cars. In fact, with less than two thousand residents, and a landmass less than three miles, its pharmacy with a working soda fountain, and knowing it's one of the few places left in America that still has a country doctor, all I can think of is Mr. Rogers' neighborhood as I look through the zoom lens of my camera. We traverse down the mountain without much fanfare, stopping every now and again to read more of those placards nailed to the trees. When climbing a mountain I always think about how it'll be easier coming down, but then rediscover how wrong I am as all my leg muscles work overtime to control my descend. My thighs burn, my knees want to buckle, and the pounding the soles of my feet take is relentless. We've been hiking for five hours, and are glad to get back to my Corolla. We dump our gear into the trunk, and head east on Route 2 back to Greenfield. I park behind the bank next to Scott's Mazda, and then we walk around the block to a local brewery that's known for their fish tacos as well as their beer. We both order a brown ale, but skip the fish tacos, and order instead two grass-fed beef burgers.

> city sidewalks
> a single blood-red leaf
> among the dead leaves

It's been dark all day, but now it's getting darker. We walk back to our cars. I tell Scott to give my best to Christine and the kids, and he assures me that he will. We say our goodbyes, and each begins our drive home in separate directions. I wonder what he's listening to on his ride home. I can hear the sound of his daughters' voices as he walks through his front door, can feel the warmth of his house, and envision the brightness of the kitchen as he and Christine sit together at the table, and he tells her about his day, and she tells him about hers.

I pull into my driveway and turn off the engine. I check the mailbox, but remember a moment too late that it's a holiday. I unlock the door to my small apartment, flick on the light, and there on the bed are six eyes squinting sleepily up at me.

> snow clouds quilt the sky
> three cats warming
> the warm bed

IF I HAD A HAMMER...
AND SOME NAILS...AND WOOD

I've a hankering to kiss you where it counts:
the road into the valley where I wish to build

a summer cottage. I'm ready to move out
of this apartment with its soapy windows

and fusty existence. I could clear a path
in the woods. I'd learn to use a bulldozer.

If you give the signal: blink or breathe,
I'd have an old borrowed machine idling,

coughing smoke. It may not look like much
but this rusty heart's a thundering juggernaut.

PO CHU-I GOLDEN SHOVEL TANKA

winter evening
full moon in the sky
you've been gone since may
what is it that you bring
across fields of snow

A MESSAGE TO SU DONGPO

The sky looks like the long beard
   of a dead monk.
Some say the murmuring brook
lurks inside the stone.
     I wander among blossoms
and try to shake the dream
   of your broad tongue.
The waves of flowers stretch
on and on like an ocean
    you can't swim,
       but an ocean
where you'll never drown.

TO LIFE

To the cat, I'm no more than a stepladder—a tool for looking out the window. From here on the bed, I see a scribble of branches, the occasional flash of bird, and the dusty underside of drawn-up blinds. The cat reports on ground activity. His chatters indicate the robin's return. His yowls announce that the calico next-door is all belly and paws in a patch of sun. Today, there are no big questions I'll ask or try to answer. Instead, I'll fold my hands on my chest, and tap a finger along to my neighbor's hammer as he pounds something beautiful and strong to life.

> sundown
> sunrise
> a butterfly
> opens and closes
> its wings

STUFF YOU SHOULD KNOW

I'm grateful to the editors of the following publications in which these poems, sometimes in different versions or under different titles, first appeared: Atlas Poetica, Bottle Rocket, Contemporary Haibun Online, Frogpond, Meat for Tea, Modern Haiku, Random Sampler, Ribbons (Tanka Society of America) and Naugatuck River Review.

"Sitting at A Picnic Table at The Quabbin Reservoir" was first published in the anthology, Compass Roads: Poems About the Pioneer Valley, Edited by Jane Yolen, published by Levellers Press.

Joshua Michael Stewart, is multi talented, a writer, a musician with a keen eye and a razor sharp mind. He knows from experience that the family sitcoms of loving families where everything works out before the show ends, has nothing to do with the reality of broken hearts, alcoholism and violence. He has a strong sense of tradition and brings forward what has been created before him and adding his own signature voice.   Human Error Publishing is honored to publish his work.

— Paul Richmond, Human Error Publishing

Joshua Michael Stewart's The Bastard Children of Dharma Bums is an impressive book. The first part features some of the best erasure work I have seen, effortlessly distilling the spirit of Kerouac while simultaneously thriving as its own strong, distinct modern work. Stewart is equally adept using haibun, tanka, golden shovel and free verse in the second part, which feels like a natural progression, clearing newer ground with similar ease while showcasing Stewart's strong, intuitive and versatile storytelling. I am certain that Kerouac, wherever he is, would love this book. And so will you.

— John Burroughs, Ohio Beat Poet Laureate and author of Rattle and Numb: Selected and New Poems 1992-2019.

Bastard Children of Dharma Bums by Joshua Michael Stewart is a book of poems in two distinct parts. The first part is a series of thirty-four "sculpted" poems. The author explains these are erasure poems without the erased lines, using Kerouac's novel, The Dharma Bums. Stewart has chosen and crafted the words to make surprising imagery and beautiful poems, which stand well together and on their own. I enjoyed his delightful use of verbs, such as "jump a bottle of wine," "surf the mountain" and "spend the warmth of God." Some of these poems are rich with language, some are more sparse. #26 reminds me of early James Wright with, "A mischievous boy, I tried to talk / to the fancy ladies in lawn hats. / Having to smile real nice, I felt / like a dead crow." I like the changeup of forms in both parts, from more modern/concrete work that creatively uses white space on the page, to golden shovels, to more traditionally lineated poems. In the second section of the book, entitled "The Hardest Path," there is a strong influence of Japanese form. "Nature Lesson" and "Shelburne Fire Tower" are basically series of haibun. Several poems have a Kerouacian use of extended haiku. This is Stewart's second book, and well worth adding to any quality poetry collection.

—Lori Desrosiers, author of Keeping Planes in the Air and other books from Salmon Poetry

www.ingramcontent.com/pod-product-compliance
Lightning Source LLC
Chambersburg PA
CBHW051701090426
42736CB00013B/2479